D1195088

KARATE CONTRACTIONS

By Gail Herman

Illustrated by Scott Angle

Language arts curriculum consultant: Debra Voege, M.A.

Gareth Stevens
Publishing

Please visit our web site at **www.garethstevens.com**.
For a free color catalog describing Gareth Stevens Publishing's list of
high-quality books, call 1-800-542-2595 (USA) or 1-800-387-3178 (Canada).
Gareth Stevens Publishing's fax: 1-877-542-2596

Library of Congress Cataloging-in-Publication Data

Herman, Gail, 1959–
        Karate contractions / by Gail Herman ; illustrated by Scott Angle ;
    language arts curriculum consultant : Debra Voege.
            p. cm. — (Grammar all-stars : kinds of words)
        At head of title : Grammar all-stars : kinds of words
        Includes bibliographical references and index.
        ISBN-10: 1-4339-0009-2   ISBN-13: 978-1-4339-0009-9 (lib. bdg.)
        ISBN-10: 1-4339-0151-X   ISBN-13: 978-1-4339-0151-5 (pbk.)
        1. English language—Contraction—Juvenile literature.   2. English
    language—Word formation—Juvenile literature.   3. English language—
    Grammar—Juvenile literature.   I. Voege, Debra.   II. Title.
    III. Title: Grammar all-stars : kinds of words.
    PE1161.H47   2009
    421'.54—dc22   2008027479

This edition first published in 2009 by
Gareth Stevens Publishing
A Weekly Reader® Company
1 Reader's Digest Road
Pleasantville, NY 10570-7000 USA

Executive Managing Editor: Lisa M. Herrington
Senior Editor: Barbara Bakowski
Creative Director: Lisa Donovan
Art Director: Ken Crossland
Publisher: Keith Garton

Printed in the United States of America

1 2 3 4 5 6 7 8 9 10 09 08

CONTENTS

Look for the **boldface** words on each page.
Then read the **KARATE KICK CLUE** that follows.

CHAPTER 1

KICKING OFF THE COMPETITION

What Are Contractions?

Sports announcer Buzz Star hurries into Kixtown Karate Center. **He's** covering the Junior Karate Tournament and **doesn't** want to miss a minute.

"Hi, Isobel!" Buzz calls out. "I hope **I'm** not late!"

"No way," says Isobel. **She's** last year's winner. Isobel is helping Buzz announce the event. "**I'm** just finishing these banners to cheer on the competitors. What do you think, Buzz?"

5

Isobel holds up the first banner. It reads: DO NOT SAY *NO, I CANNOT*. SAY *YES, I CAN!* A second banner reads: DO NOT GIVE UP! The third sign says: DO NOT JUST TRY. TRY YOUR BEST!

"Hmmm," says Buzz. "These banners are great. The words would pack more punch, though, if you used contractions."

"Contractions?" asks Isobel. **"Isn't** a contraction like a shortcut? A shorter way of writing or saying something?"

"That's right!" Buzz says. "A contraction is just one word, made by combining two other words and using an apostrophe."

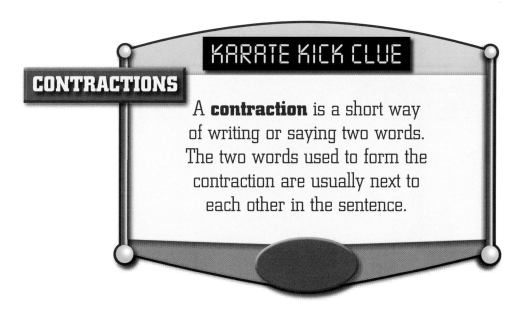

KARATE KICK CLUE

CONTRACTIONS

A **contraction** is a short way of writing or saying two words. The two words used to form the contraction are usually next to each other in the sentence.

Buzz points to the first banner. "How would you change this?"

"**DON'T** SAY *NO, I* **CAN'T**. SAY *YES, I CAN!*" Isobel smiles. "Hey! That *is* better!" Quickly, she changes the banner. **DON'T** GIVE UP! she writes for the next one. Then, **DON'T** JUST TRY. TRY YOUR BEST!

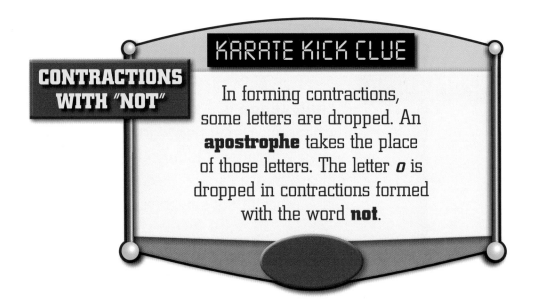

KARATE KICK CLUE

CONTRACTIONS WITH "NOT"

In forming contractions, some letters are dropped. An **apostrophe** takes the place of those letters. The letter *o* is dropped in contractions formed with the word **not**.

Isobel and Buzz hang the new banners. "What should we do with these old banners?" Buzz asks, holding one end. Isobel takes the other end.

Just then, a boy runs between them. *Ripppp!* The banners tear in half.

"Freddy Fuss!" his mother calls. "Come back here!"

"No!" Freddy shouts, stamping his foot. "I **don't** like karate! I **don't** want to watch. I **don't**! I **don't**!"

"See?" Buzz says with a laugh. "That boy is using contractions. He sounds like he means business!"

"Please, Freddy?" his mom pleads.

"I **won't** watch the tournament. I **won't**. I **won't**!"

"Freddy has no choice!" Isobel tells Buzz. "The tournament is about to start!"

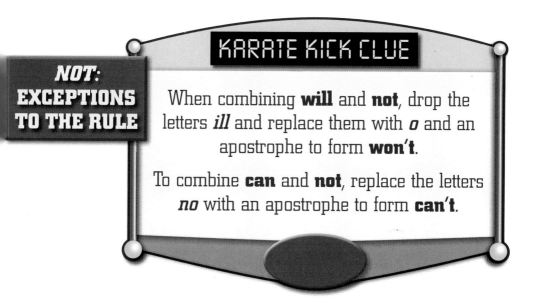

NOT: **EXCEPTIONS TO THE RULE**

KARATE KICK CLUE

When combining **will** and **not**, drop the letters *ill* and replace them with *o* and an apostrophe to form **won't**.

To combine **can** and **not**, replace the letters *no* with an apostrophe to form **can't**.

CHAPTER 2

ROUND ONE: THEY'RE OFF!
Contractions With Nouns, Pronouns, and Verbs

"This is Buzz Star for P-L-A-Y TV, reporting live from the Kixtown Junior Karate Tournament," Buzz announces. "**I'm** glad **you've** joined us to watch these karate kids kick up their heels and show their stuff. With me is Isobel Taft. **She's** last year's all-around champ. Isobel, tell our viewers about the competition."

"Sure, Buzz. The kids are getting ready for the first round: kata. In karate, kata is a routine of punches and kicks in the air."

"Participants will act as if **they're** defending themselves," Isobel explains. "But **they'll** have no opponents!"

"Here come the first three competitors, all green belts," Buzz says. He looks at Isobel. "**You're** a brown belt, right?"

Isobel nods. "Yes, **I'm** a brown belt. Students get different-colored belts as they gain new skills. Beginners wear a white belt. The black belt is for the most advanced students. Maybe next year, **I'll** be a black belt!"

"First up is Paula Packapunch," Buzz says. "Paula bows to the judges. Now **she's** ready!"

"Paula crosses her arms to protect her face," adds Isobel. "Now **she's** swinging one fist out. She quickly slides her foot in a forward movement called a lunge. **She's** definitely got the moves. **I'll** bet **Paula's** scoring plenty of points!"

"**Paula's** punching first with one hand, then the other," Buzz comments. "She gives a flying kick, then a hook kick with her left. **She's** going into a crouch. Whew! **Paula's** done. **She'll** bow to the judges."

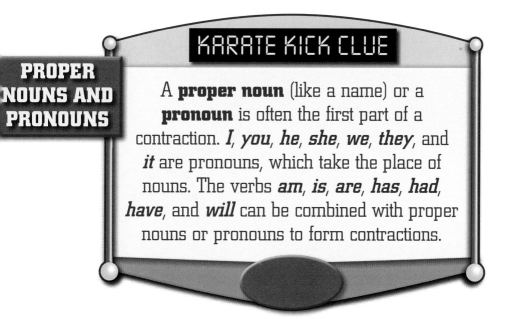

PROPER NOUNS AND PRONOUNS

KARATE KICK CLUE

A **proper noun** (like a name) or a **pronoun** is often the first part of a contraction. *I, you, he, she, we, they,* and *it* are pronouns, which take the place of nouns. The verbs *am, is, are, has, had, have,* and *will* can be combined with proper nouns or pronouns to form contractions.

"**Wasn't** Paula great? Next up is Bert Bigblock," Isobel continues. "He **doesn't** seem nervous at all. He changes speeds—fast, then slow, then fast. Now he raises his arms for a move called Unsu."

Buzz wrinkles his forehead. "I **don't** know what that word means, Isobel. Our viewers probably **aren't** familiar with it, either. Can you explain?"

"Sure, Buzz. *Unsu* means *cloud hands*. It is an advanced kata with many complex hand moves."

Buzz takes over. "Finally, Harry Hand steps onto the mat. He punches right, left, right, left. His moves **weren't** very difficult. His stance was low, though, and he changed directions quickly. Harry should win points there."

17

"*Kiai!*"

"Uh-oh!" says Isobel. "That was a karate shout from the audience. It came from Freddy Fuss!"

Buzz looks worried. "Harry **wasn't** expecting that noise. His concentration is broken. Will he get it back?"

"Yes!" cries Isobel. "Harry **doesn't** give up. He raises his leg for a roundhouse kick. He bows!"

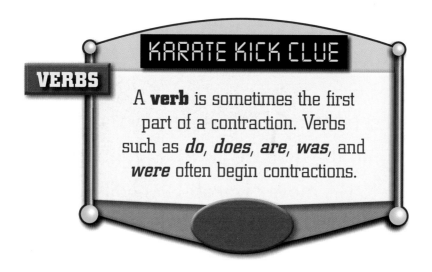

KARATE KICK CLUE

VERBS

A **verb** is sometimes the first part of a contraction. Verbs such as *do*, *does*, *are*, *was*, and *were* often begin contractions.

Buzz turns to Isobel. "You're using a lot of contractions, Isobel."

She smiles. "Right. Contractions make it easy to speak quickly and get in all the action!"

19

CHAPTER 3

ROUND TWO: WHO'S THE WINNER?

Confusing Contractions

"Welcome back, karate fans," Buzz announces. "Round two is a part of the competition called kumite."

Isobel adds, "That means sparring, Buzz. Two people face each other. They win points for punching and kicking."

"That sounds rough, Isobel," Buzz says.

"Well, they strike with speed and power," Isobel admits. "However, they stop at the moment just before contact."

"Here come Harry and Paula," Buzz tells the audience. "**Paula's** bowing to the judges. Now she turns to bow to Harry. But wait! **Harry's** bowing to the trophy table instead of the judges. Now he is bowing to Freddy Fuss instead of Paula!"

"Oops! **Harry's** face looks red," says Isobel. "He realizes he was confused."

"Contractions can be confusing, too, Isobel," says Buzz. "Sometimes, they are mistaken for possessive noun forms."

"I learned about possessives in school. A possessive noun uses an apostrophe and the letter *s* to show who or what owns something," Isobel explains.

"Exactly!" Buzz says. "***Harry's*** *green belt* means the green belt belongs to Harry. But ***Harry's*** *a green belt* means that Harry *is* a green belt."

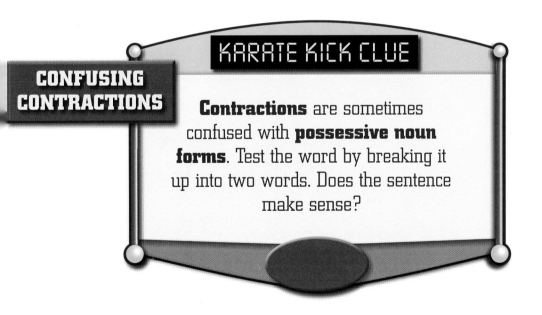

CONFUSING CONTRACTIONS

KARATE KICK CLUE

Contractions are sometimes confused with **possessive noun forms**. Test the word by breaking it up into two words. Does the sentence make sense?

"So, Buzz, **who's** going to win?" Isobel asks.

"That choice is up to the judges," Buzz replies. "They will decide **whose** performance was best in each part of the competition. **It's** anyone's guess!"

"Kumite helps develop speed, strength, and power," Isobel continues. "Kumite is also known for **its** control and discipline."

Buzz takes over. "Paula goes into a roundhouse kick, then a sidekick. Harry blocks with a back kick. **They're** evenly matched here. **Their** skill is amazing!"

"**You're** right, Buzz," Isobel says. "Keep **your** eyes on the action. Now Paula surprises Harry with a back fist."

MORE CONFUSING CONTRACTIONS

Contractions are sometimes confused with **possesive pronouns**, such as *whose*, *its*, and *your*.

"And the tournament is over!" Buzz turns to Isobel. "**You're** announcing the winners, right?"

Isobel looks at the judges' scores. "In the kata competition, Bert Bigblock takes top honors."

The audience claps.

"In the kumite competition, the winner is Paula Packapunch."

Everyone cheers.

"Finally, **I'll** announce the winner of this year's Spirit Trophy," Isobel says. "It goes to the competitor **who's** shown great sportsmanship. **It's** Harry Hand!"

"Yes! Yes! Yes!" someone shouts.

Buzz and Isobel look to see **who's** making the noise. **It's** Freddy Fuss.

"I want to try karate! I want to do it like Harry!"

Isobel kneels beside him. "You know, Freddy, karate **isn't** about winning trophies. **It's** about discipline, concentration, and respect. **That's** why we bow."

Freddy nods, a serious look on his face.

"Well, then," says Isobel, "it seems to me that **you're** ready for karate!"

"And it seems to me, Isobel, that **you'll** be a great sensei someday," Buzz says.

"What does that mean?" asks Freddy.

"A teacher!" says Buzz.

Freddy grins. "If **Isobel's** teaching karate, sign me up!"

Buzz laughs. "While Freddy is signing up, **we'll** sign off. Remember, everyone: **Don't** give up!"

KARATE KICK CLUE

TEST YOUR SKILLS

How many **contractions** can you find on pages 26 to 29?

BUZZ STAR PLAYS BY THE RULES!

 A **contraction** is a short way of writing or saying two words. The two words used to form the contraction are usually next to each other.
Example: You are a brown belt. → **You're** a brown belt.

 In a **question**, the words that make up the contraction are <u>not</u> next to each other.
Example: Why **was** she **not** ready? → Why **wasn't** she ready?

 In **forming contractions**, some letters are dropped. An apostrophe takes the place of those letters.
Examples: are not → aren't   do not → don't   will not → won't

 A **proper noun** (like a name) or a **pronoun** is often the first part of a **contraction**.
Examples: Harry is going. → **Harry's** going.
I am a brown belt. → **I'm** a brown belt.

 A **verb** is sometimes the first part of a contraction.
Example: He **does not** seem nervous. → He **doesn't** seem nervous.

 Contractions are sometimes confused with **possessive noun forms**. Test the word by breaking it up into two words. Does the sentence make sense?
Examples: Harry's bowing to the trophy table. → **Harry is** bowing to the trophy table. (yes)
Harry's face looks red. → **Harry is** face looks red. (no)

 Contractions are sometimes confused with **possessive pronouns**.
Examples: Who's going to win this tournament? (contraction of **who is**)
Whose performance was best? (possessive pronoun that means "belonging to whom")

ALL-STAR ACTIVITY

Isobel helped write a brochure for next year's tournament.
On a piece of paper, **list the contractions** in this brochure.

CALLING ALL KARATE KIDS! COME TO THE NEXT JUNIOR KARATE TOURNAMENT!

It's the best karate tournament around! You won't want to miss it! We're giving out awards and trophies. You'll enjoy refreshments, too!

So step up to the mat and take a bow! It's fun, fast, and fantastic!

Who'll be there? Everyone's invited. The tournament isn't only for skilled competitors.

Don't miss out on the excitement! Sign up now, and you've saved your spot. You're in for a thrilling event!

You can come just to watch, too! We've planned something for everyone to enjoy. You can't find a better way to spend the day!

Meet last year's winners. They'll show their best moves. They're also available to pose for photos and to sign autographs.

Place: Kixtown Karate Center
Cost: Adults $10, children $5
Doors open at 9 A.M. Don't be late!

All-Star Challenge

Write the words that make up each contraction in the brochure.

Turn the page to check your answers and to see how many points you scored!

31

ANSWER KEY

Did you find enough contractions to earn a belt?

1–4 contractions: White Belt   **9–13** contractions: Brown Belt

5–8 contractions: Green Belt   **13–16** contractions: BLACK BELT

CONTRACTIONS

1. It's
2. won't
3. We're
4. You'll
5. It's
6. Who'll
7. Everyone's
8. isn't

9. Don't
10. you've
11. You're
12. We've
13. can't
14. They'll
15. They're
16. Don't

All-Star Challenge

1. It + is
2. will + not
3. We + are
4. You + will
5. It + is
6. Who + will
7. Everyone + is
8. is + not

9. Do + not
10. you + have
11. You + are
12. We + have
13. can + not
14. They + will
15. They + are
16. Do + not